SPORTS BRANDS

ADIDAS

BY TOM STREISSGUTH

Content Consultant
Khalid Ballouli, PhD
Associate Professor
College of Hospitality, Retail and Sport Management
University of South Carolina

Essential Library
An Imprint of Abdo Publishing
abdobooks.com

ABDOBOOKS.COM

Published by Abdo Publishing, a division of ABDO, PO Box 398166, Minneapolis, Minnesota 55439. Copyright © 2023 by Abdo Consulting Group, Inc. International copyrights reserved in all countries. No part of this book may be reproduced in any form without written permission from the publisher. Essential Library™ is a trademark and logo of Abdo Publishing.

Printed in the United States of America, North Mankato, Minnesota.
052022
092022

THIS BOOK CONTAINS RECYCLED MATERIALS

Cover Photo: Gustavo Garello/AP Images
Interior Photos: Chiara Sakuwa/Shutterstock Images, 4–5; Charles Guerin/Abaca Press/Sipa USA/AP Images, 9; Angelika Warmuth/Picture Alliance/DPA/AP Images, 11; ASA/Picture Alliance/Getty Images, 13; Underwood Archives/Archive Photos/Getty Images, 14–15; Ullstein Bild/Getty Images, 17, 27; Shutterstock Images, 19, 40–41, 44, 72, 89, 92–93; Popperfoto/Getty Images, 22; Everett Collection/Shutterstock Images, 24–25; Sueddeutsche Zeitung Photo/Alamy, 31; Jack Garofalo/Paris Match Archive/Getty Images, 33; AP Images, 36; Garett Fisbeck/AP Images, 39; Lennox McLendon/AP Images, 46; Sallehudin Ahmad/Shutterstock Images, 49; Daniel Karmann/Picture Alliance/DPA/AP Images, 50; Werner Baum/Picture Alliance/DPA/Newscom, 52–53; Frank Boxler/AP Images, 55; Marcio Jose Sanchez/AP Images, 58; Aaron Doster/Cal Sport Media/AP Images, 62–63; Nicolò Campo/Sipa USA/AP Images, 65; Steven Senne/AP Images, 68; Sulastri Sulastri/Shutterstock Images, 70–71; T. Schneider/Shutterstock Images, 75; Sebastian Frej/Alamy, 77; Brauner/Ullstein Bild/Getty Images, 80–81; Tony Duffy/Allsport/Getty Images Sport Classic/Getty Images, 83; Lang Shuchen/Imagine China/AP Images, 87; Krisztian Bocsi/Bloomberg/Getty Images, 97

Editor: Arnold Ringstad
Series Designer: Sarah Taplin

Library of Congress Control Number: 2021951549
Publisher's Cataloging-in-Publication Data
Names: Streissguth, Tom, author.
Title: Adidas / by Tom Streissguth.
Description: Minneapolis, Minnesota : Abdo Publishing, 2023 | Series: Sports brands | Includes online resources and index.
Identifiers: ISBN 9781532198113 (lib. bdg.) | ISBN 9781098271763 (ebook)
Subjects: LCSH: Clothing and dress--Juvenile literature. | Adidas AG--Juvenile literature. | Sport clothes industry--Juvenile literature. | Brand name products--Juvenile literature.
Classification: DDC 338.7--dc23

CONTENTS

CHAPTER ONE
THE HOME OF POSSIBILITIES 4

CHAPTER TWO
THE STARTING LINE 14

CHAPTER THREE
WARTIME DEFEAT, OLYMPIC VICTORIES 24

CHAPTER FOUR
NEW SHOES, NEW STYLES 40

CHAPTER FIVE
WORKING WITH ATHLETES. 52

CHAPTER SIX
ON THE ADIDAS TEAM. .62

CHAPTER SEVEN
REACHING OUT TO CONSUMERS 70

CHAPTER EIGHT
CONTROVERSIES AND CHALLENGES 80

CHAPTER NINE
MARKETING THREE STRIPES. 92

ESSENTIAL FACTS	100	INDEX	110
GLOSSARY	102	ABOUT THE AUTHOR	112
ADDITIONAL RESOURCES	104	ABOUT THE CONSULTANT	112
SOURCE NOTES	106		

CHAPTER ONE

THE HOME OF POSSIBILITIES

It's a warm September day, and people are waiting patiently in front of a vast new store. It's a grand opening, a major event even in the huge and important city of New Delhi, India. The shoppers are surrounded by a familiar design featuring three parallel white stripes.

For Adidas, nothing more needs to be shown. The company's logo is famous all over the world, and the brand has millions of loyal customers. They're ready to buy just about any new line of shoes or clothing the company produces—including here in Connaught Place, in the bustling heart of India's capital.

Adidas dubbed its first flagship store in India the Home of Possibilities. Here the

> Adidas's flagship stores around the globe are where the company shows off its latest products to devoted fans of the brand.

GAME ON!

Adidas's largest flagship store is on busy Fifth Avenue in midtown Manhattan. The four-story store in the heart of New York City is designed to look like a high school stadium, with spaces imitating locker rooms, bleacher sections, batting cages, and workout rooms. Overhead, the neon lighting is shaped into the lines of a basketball court. Stadium seating is available at the front, and a tunnel entrance makes customers feel like they're marching with teammates out onto a grassy field or hardwood court.

The store offers a 360-degree virtual-reality presentation on new sneakers. For runners, an app called Run Genie uses data from sensors to analyze gait and recommends the right shoe. There are tracks where buyers can take a pair of spikes for a test run, and fitting rooms are available for trying on clothes. The whole space is designed to showcase how sports fashion and products can help athletes improve their game.

company featured anything its retail customers might dream of and some things they couldn't even imagine. Covering almost 6,000 square feet (560 sq m), the store features a variety of interactive displays that customers can use to explore products and fashion trends.[1] There are screens on the walls and on the ceilings showing athletes in motion wearing the latest in Adidas gear.

Sunil Gupta is a brand director at Adidas India. Remarking on the grand opening, he explained, "We have brought all the best that our brand can offer in an unparalleled way, bringing a global shopping experience to India under one roof. Our aim is to rethink the physical experience by providing consumers with a unique shopping experience through innovation, creativity and design."[2]

GOING LOCAL

In its marketing and in its company stores, Adidas promotes sustainability and care for the environment. The floor of the Home of Possibilities is made of carbon tiles produced from recycled materials. Many of the products on display are made from plastic waste collected from the oceans and then recycled.

One slogan the company uses is "Global Plus Local."[3] The New Delhi store features not only the brand's internationally famous products but also work from local artists and craftspeople. Many of the wall and ceiling screens feature Indian athletes. Customers can order shirts and shoes customized with their own names and faces.

An entire floor is dedicated to soccer, the most popular sport in the world and a key focus for Adidas throughout the company's history. The latest lines and models of basketball shoes are available as well. Yeezy shoes from rapper Kanye West's signature line are available, along with the latest Adidas products from designer Stella McCartney. Ivy Park, the fashion line founded by global superstar Beyoncé, wins major attention—and sales.

WINNING A CONTINENT

Adidas and its rivals compete to be the outfitter for the elite soccer teams of Europe. They pay huge sums of money to be affiliated with some of the biggest names in sports. These partnerships are subject to change when the right business deal comes along. In Spain, FC Barcelona wears the American brand Nike, while Adidas supplies rival Real Madrid. In Italy, Juventus is an Adidas team, while AC Milan wears Puma, and Inter wears Nike. And among top English teams, Adidas equips Manchester United, Nike has Liverpool and Chelsea, and Manchester City wears Puma.

South America is a different story. Adidas dominates the continent, dressing the national teams of Argentina, Colombia, and Chile. For club teams, Adidas has the two top teams in Chile and Argentina, and it has more elite partners in Brazil than its rivals do. Soccer fans trace this dominance to the 2014 World Cup, played that year in Brazil. Adidas was the sponsor for winner Germany and runner-up Argentina. It provided outfits for the referees and ball kids as well as the official ball for all the matches.

REACHING YOUNG SHOPPERS

In 2021, the same year the New Delhi flagship store opened, Beyoncé and legendary Black cowboy/actor Glynn Turman introduced Ivy Park Rodeo. This new western-themed line of clothing, shoes, and accessories combined rugged western style with flashy urban chic.

The new partnership involving stars from the world of entertainment represents an idea very important to Adidas: the company is no longer just about sports and athletes. When it was founded in 1949, Adidas sold its soccer and track shoes only in the European market. By 2022, it was a global

> Beyoncé is one of many celebrities who have forged branding partnerships with Adidas.

fashion label, with products selling on every continent but Antarctica.

Adidas has also developed a trendy image to appeal to younger shoppers. Reaching and keeping this market is essential for any clothing or shoe brand. It creates long-lasting loyalty among people who will buy the company's products throughout their lives. Setting fashion trends also means expanding beyond a narrow market, such as athletes and their teams.

DRESSING THE CHAMP

Adidas was a pioneer in athletic endorsements. It has hired thousands of athletes to wear its products in Adidas advertisements and while competing in their sports. In the 1980s, the idea expanded to sports played just for entertainment. Adidas asked actor Sylvester Stallone to wear an Adidas three-stripe warm-up suit in the boxing movie *Rocky IV*. In exchange, it agreed to supply Stallone with free shoes.

BRAND BOOSTERS

A key to the marketing success of Adidas is sponsorship and endorsements. Having famous people promoting its products has boosted Adidas's sales into the billions, making it the number two athletic apparel and shoe company in the world after Nike. This approach is nothing new for Adidas. The company has had well-known athletes wear its products for much of its history. It also supported teams, which then wore the Adidas logo on their jerseys. As television became more accessible, more and more people could see the company's name and logo in this way.

In the 1980s, sponsorship went beyond athletes and teams. With its song "My Adidas," the rap group Run-DMC celebrated Adidas as an important urban shoe trend. When Adidas partnered with the group, the era of modern sports marketing began. The company offered paid endorsement deals to musicians, actors, models, and fashion designers.

> *Adidas has been dressing Olympic athletes for many decades.*

ADIDAS NOW

Paid endorsements were unheard of in the shoe business when Adidas started out. The company has its early roots in a small workshop in a German village. Its founder, Adi Dassler, understood shoemaking and had an even greater talent for marketing. He saw the benefits of athletes wearing his products in front of a big audience. In 1928, he first brought this idea to the biggest athletic stage in the world, the Olympic Games.

Since that time, Adidas has grown into a major apparel business. It has also become a global conglomerate, buying and selling smaller brands such as Salomon, TaylorMade, Rockport, and Reebok. Smart marketing campaigns played a key role in Adidas's growth.

The company's path to its modern success wasn't always smooth. It started in a bitter dispute between Adi and his brother Rudolf. In the 1990s, poor management nearly drove Adidas into bankruptcy. Adidas has also faced controversy in its business practices and its association with the former Nazi government of Germany. Environmental concerns and labor practices also have led to negative press in an image-conscious industry.

The company's leadership has adapted to changing times, when running a business means carefully managing a brand. One area of focus is customizing products to suit individual customers' tastes. Another is environmental sustainability, along with attention to working conditions in the factories that make its products. Through these changes and challenges Adidas has managed to keep growing and competing. It remains at or near the top of the shoe market everywhere it does business.

THE BALL SEEN 'ROUND THE WORLD

PRODUCT SPOTLIGHT

Soccer met the age of television in the 1960s. League matches and tournaments in Europe and Latin America drew huge audiences. There was just one problem: on a big soccer field, with 22 players rushing around and into each other, it was hard for viewers in the age of small, black-and-white TVs to see and follow the ball.

Adidas offered a solution with the Telstar, a new ball designed by Danish goalkeeper Eigil Nielsen. Named for an orbital satellite, this ball had a design of 12 black pentagons and 20 white hexagons. In the language of geometry, the design was a truncated icosahedron. When a player kicked the ball forward, its black pentagons spun rapidly, making it easy for players, refs, fans in the stands, and a television audience to see. Although Adidas has designed dozens of flashy soccer balls since the 1960s and sold millions of them around the world, people still imagine the Telstar when they think of soccer.

CHAPTER TWO

THE STARTING LINE

Lina Radke and eight competitors took their places at the starting line. The date was August 2, 1928, and the event was the 800-meter final at the Olympic Games in Amsterdam, Holland. For the first time in Olympic history, women were competing in track-and-field events. The starter's gun went off. As the crowd roared, the athletes sprang from the line.

Marie Dollinger of Germany took the lead. She was the favorite to win the gold medal. But on the final turn, Dollinger's big lead disappeared. With a burst of speed, Radke, her teammate, edged to the front. Kinue Hitomi of Japan and Inga Gentzel of Sweden were catching up as well.

> Runner Lina Radke was among the earliest world-class athletes to use shoes created by the future founder of Adidas.

The women were running hard down the final straight, straining to reach the finish line fastest. But Radke, at the front of the pack, had an edge. Her shoes had steel spikes that gripped the track and allowed her to push hard against the ground. With the help of these spikes, Radke crossed the line first, achieving a new world-record time of two minutes and 16.8 seconds.[1] In doing so, she became the first athlete to win an Olympic race in shoes made by the Dassler brothers.

SHOE BROTHERS

Adolf Dassler was born in 1900 in the small town of Herzogenaurach, Germany. Nicknamed Adi, he loved athletics and took part in football, skiing, and track. He joined the German military during World War I (1914–1918).

A SCANDALOUS FINISH

Lina Radke's 800-meter women's final at the Amsterdam Games ended in controversy. Several women dropped to the ground after the finish. It's not uncommon for runners to be exhausted after a race. However, a reporter named John Tunis later claimed that five of the women "collapsed" while five others dropped out before the finish.[2]

The reporting was false, as none of the runners abandoned the race. But the International Olympic Committee (IOC) believed Tunis. A scandal erupted over concern for supposedly frail female runners. The IOC dropped the women's 800-meter run from the Olympic program. Women were not permitted to run a race longer than 200 meters until the 1960 Olympic Games in Rome, Italy.

> *Adi Dassler eventually turned his local shoemaking operation into a global brand.*

After the war, Adi showed an interest in sports equipment, especially shoes. He loved tinkering with shoe designs, shaping wooden lasts, and treating leather to make the fastest and most comfortable running shoe possible. Along with his older brother Rudolf, Adi registered the Dassler Brothers Sports Shoe Factory in the summer of 1924. The company began in a small workshop they converted from a laundry room in the back of their family home.

Germany faced economic hardship and scarcity after World War I, so the Dasslers used scavenged materials such as parachutes and army helmets to construct their earliest shoes. Eventually they used machinery that cut material they could assemble. When electricity to run a cutting machine was unavailable, the Dassler brothers used generators powered by bicycles.

The company grew slowly. There was a market for athletic shoes after the war, even though many people in Germany lived in harsh poverty. In 1926, the Dasslers moved out of the family washroom and into a bigger factory space. Demand for sports shoes was growing as the German economy slowly recovered from the country's defeat in World War I. In this important year, the Dassler brothers had 25 workers making 100 pairs of shoes a day.[3]

ROOTS

At first the Dassler family trained Adi to be a baker. He also had a chance to carry on the family's traditional occupation of weaver. But Dassler preferred to tinker and invent athletic gear at a shoemaker's workbench, and he was a dedicated school athlete. He was also in a natural place to enter the shoe business. Herzogenaurach, the Dasslers' hometown, had a long tradition as a center for shoemaking. In 1922, for example, it boasted 112 shoemakers in a population of just 3,500 people.[4]

> *Adding spikes to running shoes has long been seen as a way to improve athletes' performance.*

THE SPIKED SHOE

Plenty of family-owned companies in Germany used small workshops to make shoes at the time. Running shoes were simple footwear made of leather or canvas uppers fused to rubber soles. Athletes paid little heed to the brand names.

Adi Dassler had an idea for the shoe industry. Each kind of sport would require a specially designed shoe to improve athletes' performance. Adi approached the problem of running shoes. He asked his friend, blacksmith Fritz Zehlein, to design steel spikes to be attached to the bottoms of running shoes. Spikes would give the athlete more grip on the running surface. This would allow a strong runner to run a little faster than the competition. Spikes had been used in shoes before. But Dassler improved the design and tailored it specifically for runners.

Creating a new type of shoe was one matter. But the Dasslers also had to convince athletes to try them. If those athletes became champions, word of the shoes they were wearing might spread. If so, the Dasslers hoped their shoes would gain a reputation for winning and more athletes would put them on, lace them up, and win. Success for athletes could lead to success for the company.

SNEAKERS

Rubber shoe soles were invented in the 1800s. Rubber began to replace leather in shoes made by factory assembly lines as the factories replaced individual shoe cobblers. Those who wore the rubber soles noticed that they had a special quality: they were very quiet. In fact, these shoes made it easier than ordinary leather street shoes to sneak around silently and take people by surprise. That's how rubber-soled shoes got their nickname: sneakers. Since then, people have come up with plenty of other words for athletic shoes, including *trainers* and *kicks*.

SHOES IN THE SPOTLIGHT

The young company waited for a major sporting event. When the Dasslers were starting out in the 1920s, the world's biggest athletic competition was the Olympic Games. Making a splash at the Olympics could win their shoes global publicity.

With the 1928 Olympics in Amsterdam approaching, Adi called on Lina Radke, a member of the German women's track team. He offered Radke a new type of shoe for the competition. She agreed to try the spiked Dassler shoes. Then she wore them on her world-record run in Amsterdam. The Dasslers next offered their shoes to Josef Waitzer, coach of the German national track-and-field team. He accepted. Athletes again wore the shoes at the 1932 Olympics in Los Angeles, California, and

HOW THE STRIPES BEGAN

The three stripes that have symbolized Adidas shoes for almost a century have their roots in the shoe crafted by Adi Dassler for Lina Radke for the 1928 Olympic Games in Amsterdam. Dassler used a method of stitching a vertical stripe on the sides of the shoe. The stripe was there to strengthen the upper part of the shoe and allow it to fit more snugly around the foot. It also helped the shoe last a little longer.

The stripe was in a contrasting white color, allowing it to stand out against the brown leather of the shoe's upper. But it wasn't yet used as a logo or marketing device. Over the years, Dassler experimented with different shapes for the vertical stripe; he also tried using two, four, and six stripes. Finally, in 1948, he settled on a set of three white stripes, which became the Adidas trademark.

▶ *Owens wore Dassler's spiked shoes during his incredible performance at the Berlin Olympics.*

at the 1936 Summer Games in Berlin, Germany. As a result of all this exposure, the Dassler shoes gained a nationwide German market.

A WIN IN BERLIN

Berlin, as the capital of Germany, was the seat of the Nazi government of Germany in the 1930s. The Nazi regime was led by dictator Adolf Hitler. Hitler believed German victories in athletics would prove to the world the superiority of the German race. Success also would signify that Germany had moved past its defeat in World War I and had regained its status as a world power, he believed.

In addition to providing shoes to the German team, the Dasslers offered the use of their spiked shoes to an American athlete, Jesse Owens. Owens was a Black runner from Ohio. He accepted the Dasslers' offer of steel-spiked running shoes. This made him the first Black athlete in history to gain a corporate sponsor.

Owens outran the Germans and everybody else in the 100-meter dash. In this event, he equaled the world-record time of 10.3 seconds.[5] He won a total of four gold medals, also besting the competition in the long jump, the 200-meter dash, and the 4x100-meter relay. His time in the 200-meter race and his distance in the long jump were world records. Owens became an Olympic legend for his feats, and he accomplished them while wearing Dassler shoes.

CHAPTER THREE

WARTIME DEFEAT, OLYMPIC VICTORIES

Three years after the Berlin Olympics, another war broke out in Europe. World War II (1939–1945) began when Germany invaded Poland in 1939. In the next year, Germany invaded France and the Netherlands. The war later spread across Europe and to North Africa and Asia. Germany, Japan, and Italy, known as the Axis powers, were on one side of the war. The other side, the Allies, included the United Kingdom, the United States, the Soviet Union, and China. Many German athletes joined the armed forces. The German government declared an all-out, national effort to win the war. Its leaders canceled many civilian sporting events and shut down sports leagues.

> *The outbreak of World War II eventually triggered the feud that would divide the Dassler brothers forever.*

Private companies were ordered to make material and weapons for the war effort. Rudolf Dassler believed the Dassler Brothers Sports Shoe Factory could produce boots for the army. But Germany's leaders had other ideas. Instead of footwear, the Dasslers were ordered to make anti-tank weapons.

POSTWAR DIVISIONS

The Dasslers cooperated with the regime. They knew that refusing would probably mean the end of their business. It could also land them in prison. Adi was drafted into the military in 1940, where he was a radio operator for the air force. In January of the next year, he was released from military service, and the company was ordered to produce athletic shoes for the military. Rudolf was drafted in 1943. Their wartime dealings with the German government would cause tension and arguments between the brothers.

According to Dassler family legends, the bitter feud between Rudolf and Adi Dassler reached its breaking point one night toward the end of the war. With Allied bombers flying over their hometown, the family escaped to a bomb shelter built on their property.

> *Following the war, the split between the two brothers would lead Adi to strike out on his own.*

Rudolf and his wife were the first to reach the shelter, with Adi and his family following soon afterward. When Adi spotted his brother, he muttered, "Here are the bloody b— again."[1] Rudolf didn't take the remark well. Although Adi always claimed that he said "bloody b—" to mean the Allied pilots, Rudolf felt sure the words were directed at him and his wife. For this, he never forgave Adi.

A NEW MARKET FOR SHOES

World War II came to a bloody and violent end in Herzogenaurach. The town suffered bombing raids and lost many of its young men at the battlefronts. The Dasslers were also affected by the war. The brothers argued often over their relations with the Nazi government and their war service. In 1943 their shoe business had to shut down altogether.

But their luck turned as American troops swept through in 1945. The US forces took over a German air base at Herzogenaurach, and the American soldiers stationed there were a very receptive market for sports shoes. After finding out that the Dasslers had supplied the shoes Jesse Owens wore at the 1936 Olympics, they started ordering Dasslers for their baseball and basketball squads. This was key in helping the business survive the tough postwar years.

Germany lost the war in the spring of 1945. The country was put under occupation by the Allied armies of the United Kingdom, France, the Soviet Union, and the United States. The occupation government put Adi on trial. Prosecutors accused him of profiting from the war and from his connections with the Nazi Party.

Rudolf did nothing to help his brother. He declared that Adi had purposely worked with the Nazis. Rudolf also stated that he had opposed the production of war material but couldn't prevent it, as he had been drafted into the German army. However, the mayor of Herzogenaurach came to Adi's rescue. He testified that Adi had protected him from persecution by the Nazis.

Adi escaped a prison sentence, but the war had caused an angry rift between the brothers. Their rivalry ended the

Dassler Brothers Sports Shoe Factory. Rudolf started his own shoe business, known as Puma, in 1948. In 1949, Adi Dassler founded his own new company, combining the first parts of *Adolf* and *Dassler* to come up with the Adidas name. This new start gave him an opportunity to pursue his own vision for the sports shoe business and to run a company based on the slogan he used: "Innovate, don't imitate."[2]

MIRACLE AT THE WORLD CUP

Following World War II, Germany was divided. The areas the United States, the United Kingdom, and France had occupied became West Germany, and the Soviet Union's area of occupation became East Germany. In 1954, a young West German soccer team traveled to Switzerland to compete in the World Cup. Although West

DIVIDED BY A RIVER

Adidas and Puma have been rivals ever since they were founded by the Dassler brothers in the late 1940s. But Rudolf and Adolf Dassler both felt close ties to their hometown of Herzogenaurach, Germany. Neither would move his company to a bigger city. Adidas set up shop north of the Aurach River, the stream that runs through the middle of Herzogenaurach. Rudolf's Puma had its factory on the river's south bank. The humble Aurach has separated the two big shoe companies ever since.

Team Adidas and team Puma have their own schools, restaurants, and bakeries. Most townspeople join one side or the other, often depending on the loyalty of their parents and families. The sports shoe business created one of the world's longest-lasting competitions in the town of Herzogenaurach.

Germany was not rated very highly, the team played well. During the group stage, it faced a powerful team from Hungary that had racked up 30 straight wins. The West Germans lost the match by a score of 8–3. However, they still advanced to the knockout round and then won two games to reach the final.

The final took place on July 4, a rainy day at Bern's Wankdorf Stadium. Once again West Germany faced the fearsome Hungarians. The pitch was muddy and slippery, making it hard for the players to stop, pivot, or reverse direction. But West Germany had a secret weapon in Adi Dassler's Argentina shoes. This model had screw-in studs on its soles. The studs could be changed out for stronger ones designed for slippery conditions. While the Hungarians, with their ordinary shoes, slipped and fell in the mud, the Germans in their Dasslers ran swiftly and steadily, and they didn't seem to mind the bad conditions.

This was the first World Cup final to be shown on television. Within ten minutes of the start, Hungary scored two goals. Everyone watching on television and in the stadium was certain West Germany would lose. But the Germans came back with two goals of their own to tie the match. With six minutes left, Helmut Rahn scored the winner for West Germany.

> *Adi Dassler,* left, *posed with the West German national soccer team after the thrilling victory.*

The match, known in soccer history as the Miracle of Bern, went down as one of the most exciting and important soccer matches ever. It catapulted Germany to the global soccer elite, a place it has held ever since. It also put another winning spotlight on Adi Dassler's shoes.

GIVING AWAY SHOES

The 1956 Olympics in Melbourne, Australia, gave Adidas another opportunity to publicize itself. By this time, Adi's son Horst had joined the company. A smart and hard-driving natural salesman, Horst outdid his father in

ADIDAS AND THE THREE STRIPES

When Adi Dassler founded Adidas, he avoided using the two two-stripe design previously used in the partnership with his brother. But a three-stripe logo was already used by Karhu, a Finnish sports company. Karhu, like Adidas, sponsored athletes who were Olympic champions, with 15 gold-medal winners wearing its shoes at the 1952 Games in Helsinki, the capital of Finland.

Dassler sought out Karhu to clear up any confusion and avoid legal problems over the logo. The story of the deal has become legendary in the history of sporting goods. In 1952 Dassler invited directors of the Finnish company to the Adidas headquarters in Germany. During the visit, the two sides agreed that for the right to use Karhu's simple design, Adidas would pay two bottles of whiskey and a sum totaling a few thousand dollars in today's money.

seeking out new markets for their shoes.

But the Olympic Games still strictly banned any money-making promotions among its athletes. Olympians were supposed to be amateurs, competing for the love of the sport. They were not supposed to have any interest in earning money from their athletic ability. Also, according to the Olympic rules, sports advertisers could not use images that clearly identified individual Olympic athletes.

Horst came up with a solution. Instead of paying in any way to promote the company, he would simply give away spiked running shoes as "technical equipment." He claimed that track-and-field athletes needed them to get a better grip on the loose gravel of cinder tracks. The shoes, of course, carried the very visible three-striped Adidas logo on their

> Thanks to the efforts of Horst Dassler, the three stripes of Adidas were widely visible at the Melbourne Olympics.

sides. While it was hard to tell one brown leather shoe from another at a distance, the three stripes made it clear to the fans in the stands and in the television audience who the maker was.

More than 70 medal winners at the Melbourne Olympic Games wore the Adidas shoes given away by Horst Dassler. This simple marketing idea gave rise to one of the most important moments in company history. The 1956 Olympics were the first to be widely televised. The big television audience in the United States did not miss the three-stripe logo.

In California, Chris and Clifford Severn of North Hollywood had convinced the Dasslers to appoint them as local Adidas distributors. They stored the imported shoes in their garage but for a long time couldn't sell them. Nobody in the United States knew the brand, and the

ADIDAS—OR ELSE!

Adi Dassler valued brand loyalty above all else. German sprinter Armin Hary discovered this at the 1960 Olympics in Rome, Italy. Recruited by both Adidas and Puma to wear their shoes, Hary tried to play both sides. He wore a pair of Pumas to the 100-meter final, winning the event with a time of 10.2 seconds. For the awards ceremony, he switched to Adidas.

Hary may have calculated that both companies would now compete for his partnership. But Adi couldn't abide an athlete who switched sides in the middle of a competition. He banned any more Adidas deals with Hary—for life.

state of California had a policy of buying only US-made sports equipment for its high schools.

After the Melbourne Games, however, the demand for Adidas shoes exploded throughout the United States. The Severns and other distributors faced a new problem. Now the Adidas factories in Europe couldn't make shoes fast enough to keep up with the demand in the hot American market.

A CHANGE OF OWNERSHIP

At the Mexico City Olympics in 1968, Adidas added to its roster of sponsored champions. Bob Beamon, who smashed the world long-jump record, made his incredible leap in a pair of Adidas. Beamon had worn Pumas in the preliminary heats but switched to Adidas for the final.

In 1978, Adidas began going through changes. In that year, Adi Dassler died, leaving his company under the control of his wife, Käthe. His son, Horst, worked in the company's upper management. Horst went on to head the company from 1984, when his mother died, until he died in 1987. Adidas was then sold to Bernard Tapie, a French businessman.

Tapie specialized in turning around companies in financial trouble. But to do so, he took on big loans.

> *Bob Beamon's long jump in the 1968 Olympics broke a record and also gave more exposure to Adidas's three stripes.*

Within a few years, these loans got Tapie into heavy debt. The French bank Crédit Lyonnais took control of his businesses in the 1990s. The bank appointed

French businessman Robert Louis-Dreyfus as the new chief executive officer in 1993.

At this time, a new competitor across the Atlantic was giving Adidas a run for its money. Nike had its own stable of sponsored superstars, and it was drawing even with Adidas in global sales. Adidas was in for a rough patch in the highly competitive sportswear industry.

SWOOSH VERSUS STRIPES

Phil Knight, the founder of the Nike sporting goods company, sought to compete with and beat Adidas in the United States. In the 1970s, he made it his goal to outsell the expensive German shoe with his company's American models. One thing Adidas taught Knight was the importance of a simple, easy-to-recognize logo. In 1971, just after founding his company, he commissioned design student Carolyn Davidson to come up with a logo for Nike.

The result was the Swoosh, a big, curving sideways comma that made Nike gear look like it was moving at high speed, even when it was standing still. For the Swoosh, a logo that's now worth billions to the Nike company, Knight paid Davidson a grand total of $35.[3] The Swoosh and the Adidas stripes went on to dominate the sports shoe business over the next several decades.

SPORTS FOCUS

BASKETBALL

Adidas began in Europe, where in the early years it focused on soccer and track shoes for the European market. But company executives saw huge potential in the United States, where basketball was played by millions in professional, amateur, and school leagues.

Adidas began designing shoes for basketball players in the 1960s. The Superstar was Adidas's breakthrough basketball shoe. It was designed with leather uppers, giving the ankles more support than traditional canvas. This was essential for a game that demands constant pivoting and fast push-offs. The Superstar quickly replaced the Converse All-Star as the shoe of choice for hoops players.

In the 2000s, Adidas continued to innovate in basketball shoe tech. Boost technology introduced new compounds for the midsole to improve support. Shoes using Lightstrike cushioning are even lighter than Boost. These materials are designed for the fast lateral movements basketball players have to make, whether they're guarding at the three-point line or dribbling around a teammate's pick.

> *James Harden, right, is among the NBA players who have major deals with Adidas.*

Adidas offers a lot of options to suit the demands of different positions and styles of play. Basketball players can choose low-top, mid-top, or high-top shoes. They can order laced or laceless models. Players can get more comfort and support from Boost midsoles, or they can opt for greater speed and faster response from Lightstrike. Some Adidas models are specifically designed for flat feet, and others are for wide feet. Finally, there's style. The company offers a broad palette of colors and designs to suit the look each player wants.

CHAPTER FOUR

NEW SHOES, NEW STYLES

It's a busy, bustling weekend at the Twin Cities Premium Outlets in Eagan, Minnesota, where companies sell discounted clothing and promote their product lines. The Adidas shop, as usual, is attracting a big crowd from the shopping center's heavy foot traffic. Rising near the southwestern corner of the mall, the Adidas shop is not far from similar outlets operated by Nike and Puma. At the entrance are sweaters, hoodies, T-shirts, and gym bags. They all carry the Adidas name, the trefoil logo, or the famous three stripes. When you wear Adidas, there's no guessing the brand.

Farther into the store, and covering the back half, is a maze of narrow aisles stacked floor to ceiling with shoeboxes.

> *Displays at Adidas retail stores showcase the wide variety of shoe styles and colors the company offers.*

41

THE SPORTSWEAR STORE

As Adidas and the sportswear business grew through the 1990s, the company invested in a new concept in retailing: the company store. This would be a store dedicated exclusively to Adidas shoes, clothing, and sports accessories. Adidas would own and operate the store, which could promote new lines and new models of Adidas products as they came out.

Adidas took the concept a step further with its first Originals store, which opened in the trendy Mitte neighborhood of Berlin in 2001. The company developed the Originals line of sweats, hoodies, and T-shirts after the success of the company's tracksuit in the 1970s. Originals streetwear has been adopted around the world as pro athletes who promote the gear have become international superstars. Originals stores later opened in London, New York City, and Tokyo, closely tying in with the company's plan to focus on key centers of design and sports in Europe, North America, and Asia.

Individual shoes are displayed to show off the latest designs. Some of these colorful three-striped shoes are for kids, some for women, and some for men. There are shoes designed for soccer, running, tennis, and basketball. Turning the shoes over reveals a complicated design of hard rubber ridges, cushions, grooves, and spikes.

Customers inch through the store, getting a look and trying stuff on. They wander to the racks of shorts. They inspect displays of crew socks, waist packs, and water bottles. Many of them are from out of town—way out of town. When they're in the Twin Cities, thousands of foreign tourists make a trip out to this suburban outlet not far from the airport. Many of them don't want to miss the Adidas store.

SAMBAS AND STAN SMITHS

To meet the growing demand for athletic shoes, Adidas has created dozens of different designs. When the new models start catching on with consumers, the company begins to develop new looks for them. The basic shape and materials of each model remain the same, but the shoes appear in new colors and carry flashy new designs.

Starting in the 1950s, new models appeared every few years. Some of these shoes have now been dominating their markets for more than half a century. Named to honor the flamboyant style of Brazilian soccer teams, the black-and-white Samba came out in 1950. This Samba was designed as an all-weather shoe, adapted to both tropical pitches in Latin America and cold-weather fields in Europe. It was cut low, with a lightweight leather upper and a gum-rubber sole. In the 2020s, the Samba remains a familiar men's shoe around the world.

Adidas regularly updates and expands its most popular shoe lines. The Samba shoe, for example, has also become the Samba boot. A variant of the shoe has also been designed for kids.

In the 1960s, the company started associating its product lines with famous athletes. Believing tennis

players were ready to move past traditional canvas shoes, Adidas created the first leather tennis shoe in the 1960s, naming it for the French player Robert Haillet. When Haillet retired from tennis, Adidas offered the shoe and an endorsement to rising American tennis star Stan Smith.

The Stan Smith has kept the same design for the last 50 years. It's a low-cut, simply designed leather shoe in white, with different colors used for the small heel tab at the back of the foot. Adidas has made other licensing agreements, combining its name with those of other companies, celebrities, and shows to give the shoe a trendy buzz. Stan Smith

HAVE A COKE AND A CUP

Horst Dassler was one of Adidas's most inventive executives. He came up with many new ways to promote the company's products. Often called the father of sports sponsorship, he was a pioneer in the business of signing individual pro athletes to endorsements. In the 1970s, Dassler partnered with British advertising executive Patrick Nally to form the world's first sports marketing company. The two came up with the idea of company sponsorships for major sporting events. This would help the events raise the money needed to host big matches and draw big audiences.

The concept was brand-new to FIFA, the organization that runs global soccer, including the World Cup. But FIFA president João Havelange was interested in trying it. Dassler and Nally then approached Coca-Cola and convinced the company to sponsor the 1978 World Cup for the sum of $8 million.[1] Coca-Cola bought advertising rights, becoming the first exclusive worldwide sponsor of any major sporting event.

> *The Samba is among the most iconic models that Adidas makes.*

▸ Kareem Abdul-Jabbar, left, and other NBA players helped popularize Adidas's line of basketball shoes.

designs have featured *Sesame Street*'s Kermit the Frog, Miss Piggy of *The Muppet Show*, and characters from Disney's *Monsters, Inc*. In the 2000s, Adidas began making Stan Smith uppers with recycled material as a nod to the company's stated concern for sustainability and the environment.

A SUPERSTAR IS BORN

At about the same time the Stan Smith was launching and winning a big fan base among tennis stars, Adidas was marketing the new Superstar to basketball players. It was a low-top shoe with a leather upper and a shell toe. This unique rubber shell design covered the top front of the shoe, protecting the toes when someone stepped on the wearer's foot, which could happen often during a hard-fought basketball game.

Adidas introduced the Superstar after the 1969 National Basketball Association (NBA) Finals. Kareem Abdul-Jabbar and other basketball stars soon began wearing them. The shoes were a hit on urban playgrounds and in school gyms across the United States.

Adopted by many young people for everyday wear, the Superstar spread from the basketball court to the streets. It was celebrated by the rap group Run-DMC in its song "My Adidas," which came out in 1986. The group wore the shoes laceless and with the shoes' tongues hanging out whenever they performed live.

One evening in 1986, Run-DMC manager Lyor Cohen brought an Adidas executive, Angelo Anastasio, along to a concert. During the show, the group told audience members wearing Adidas to take a shoe off and hold it in the air. As Anastasio watched, thousands of people held up Adidas shoes. The group then made a video just for Adidas, in which they chanted the rap and ended with a request to "Give Us a Million Dollars!" Impressed and persuaded, the company soon offered the group a $1 million endorsement contract.[2] Run-DMC was the first nonsports entity Adidas ever signed to promote the brand. The partnership was

THE SPORT OF HOSTING

In the never-ending battle with Puma for customers and clients, Adidas had a secret weapon. This was the Auberge du Kochersberg, a lavish hunting lodge in Alsace, a hilly and wooded region of eastern France. Adidas invited athletes, coaches, and sports executives from all over the world to spend a few nights at the lodge, where they enjoyed splendid meals and sampled a glass or two from an enormous wine cellar. The most important guests stayed in big suites on the top floor and ate from gold-rimmed plates in an exclusive private dining room. Chauffeured limousines were on call to ferry guests around the region and take them on hunting trips into the nearby forests. Treated like royalty, guests never forgot a stay at the Auberge du Kochersberg. And they often repaid the favor by ordering their shoes and equipment exclusively from Adidas.

> *Adidas's Tobacco shoe has been available in a variety of colors during its rereleases over the years.*

also the start of a wave among sportswear companies to enlist fashion designers, musicians, actors, and other nonathletes as endorsers.

NEWER, STRANGER SHOES

Following up on the Superstar, Adidas came out with several more sneaker lines over the next 30 years. To compete with the famous Converse All-Star, the canvas Adidas Nizza first appeared in 1975. The eye-catching

> *The company demonstrated the flexibility of its Energy Boost line of shoes at a 2013 press conference.*

suede Tobacco shoe was introduced in 1978 and has become a popular retro style in the 2000s. The Forest Hills appeared the next year for tennis players, later growing in popularity among British and European soccer players.

Copa Mundial, another soccer shoe, has been winning awards and selling in the millions since its introduction during the 1982 World Cup. Adicolor, which appeared two years later, came with a pack of felt pens, allowing owners to customize the shoes with their own designs.

The company's cushioned Energy Boost shoes first appeared in 2013. The shoes were a response to Nike's Air shoe, which used a rubberlike substance known as ethylene-vinyl acetate (EVA) to give the wearer a cushioning layer under the feet. Adidas took the concept a step further by using a material called thermoplastic polyurethane (TPU). The Boost incorporated TPU in the form of small pellets of material welded together and blown into the shoe's midsole. This made the Boost not only cushioned but also more durable. It also provided an improved ability to store energy and then unleash it when the wearer jumps or pushes off.

GAMING THE FUTURE

Adidas has gone beyond making shoes for running, jumping, and soccer. It has even gone beyond athletic gear for amateur athletes and fitness enthusiasts. The company is now partnering with gamers in the world of e-sports. Company vice president Bjorn Jager says, "We already have musicians, artists, and athletes . . . so it just depends on the key messaging we want to put in our marketing."[3]

In 2021, Adidas partnered with G2, a squad based in Germany and one of the world's most successful e-sports teams. G2 gamers wear Adidas while competing, and the team's own designers are creating Adidas-themed lifestyle apparel for street use. "We're not talking about a team only with G2," says Jager. "We're talking about an entertainment company."[4] The partnership involves more than game-day jerseys or shoes. G2 plans to feature Adidas prominently in its podcasts, reality shows, and other game-themed entertainment.

CHAPTER FIVE

WORKING WITH ATHLETES

Adidas has been working with athletes to promote its brand since the 1920s, when it was the Dassler Brothers Sports Shoe Factory. It began with Olympic champions such as Lina Radke and Jesse Owens. It continued with the underdog West German men's soccer team in the 1950s.

Adi Dassler made friendships with many star athletes and successful coaches. He tailored Adidas products to meet their needs. He consulted with them to design new running and soccer shoes. This led to innovations that helped keep Adidas at the forefront of the competitive sports apparel industry.

> *Adi Dassler, right, shows off new shoes to German soccer players in 1974.*

STAR SHOE POWER

Adidas now has sponsorship deals with hundreds of professional athletes all over the world. These deals pay the athletes to wear Adidas shoes and gear. In return, the athletes promote the brand, helping the company sell more products. In some cases, athletes lend their names to lines of shoes or sportswear. The trend began with the Stan Smith tennis shoe, which eventually became the company's all-time best-selling shoe.

Sometimes celebrities help create the shoes too. Ciara, Snoop Dogg, and Pharrell Williams all have collaborated with Adidas on new product lines. The Yeezy Boost, named for rapper Kanye West, became a hot seller in the 2010s.

GOING SWIMMINGLY

Horst Dassler kept busy during the 1972 Summer Olympics in Munich, West Germany. On the lookout for top athletes to promote Adidas, no matter what sport they competed in, he approached US swimmer Mark Spitz. Dassler appreciated Spitz's confidence, athletic ability, and movie-star looks. But there was one obvious problem: swimmers don't wear shoes.

Still, Spitz agreed to do the best he could, which meant wearing Adidas shoes around the Olympic village and whenever he was on camera. He held up his end of the deal in the pool as well, earning a record seven gold medals. For the medal ceremonies, Dassler and Spitz hit on the idea of the swimmer bringing his Adidas Gazelles. To avoid having his baggy tracksuit pants cover the shoes, Spitz held the Gazelles up, then set them down on the podium as the anthems played.

> *Part of the deal that Beckham, right, made with Adidas included the creation of a personal logo for the soccer star's brand.*

When athletes or music stars appear in Adidas gear, millions of fans take notice.

MAJOR PLAYERS, BIG MONEY

Some of these high-profile shoe deals pay big money. Top athletes and entertainers may earn even more from the endorsements than from playing their sports. In 2003, English soccer player David Beckham signed a contract worth $160 million to promote Adidas.[1] The company bet on Beckham, knowing he had global name recognition.

Soccer superstar Lionel Messi, one of the world's best-paid athletes, also signed with Adidas. His endorsement income amounts to tens of millions of dollars per year. But for all the money invested in him, the company made a good deal. Adidas sells enormous numbers of Messi shoes, jerseys, shin guards, and other accessories. On the first day of sales of the new PSG Messi jersey in August 2021, for example, Adidas sold out its entire online stock of jerseys in 30 minutes, earning millions for both the company and the club.[2]

SPONSORS IN THE UNITED STATES

In the United States, many basketball and football players sign major endorsement contracts. For the top stars, Adidas may agree to create a signature line. This is a product that carries the name of a top star, such as Kobe Bryant or Patrick Mahomes. The athletes earn royalties on sales of their signature lines, in addition to endorsement fees. For athletes not at the top of the game, the deals are more modest.

HOW DO YOU FEEL ABOUT THAT SHOE?

Adidas is all about testing and experimenting with real athletes to figure out how to design new shoes. This work has led to breakthroughs in the materials and construction of shoes and other gear. The company also does research into feelings. Researchers have measured athletic performance in many ways, and they have found that the way athletes respond emotionally to the look and feel of a shoe can affect how well they do on the field or the court. Researcher Paul Francis explained it this way: "Every athlete wants to be better, but not many want to change. Many times, the obstacle to change isn't that they doubt the performance of the shoe, it just doesn't look good and feel good."[3]

The company will pay less money but may also offer the athlete some free merchandise.

Contracts will also establish performance terms. The contract may pay a bonus if a baseball player hits a certain batting average, for example, or a basketball player makes the NBA Finals or the All-Star Game. When athletes perform well, they have a larger spotlight on them, which in turn provides more exposure for the products they endorse.

TERMS OF THE DEAL

Visibility is the key to endorsement deals. Millions of people might watch the Adidas athlete on the field. But even off the field, that athlete can garner attention for the company. They might wear Adidas clothes while in public or in social media posts.

> **SAYING IT RIGHT**
>
> When Adi Dassler formed Adidas, his name for the company combined *Adi* and *Dassler*. As the Germans pronounce it, the nickname Adi has the stress on the first syllable. As a result, in Germany and the rest of Europe, the name *Adidas* carries the same stress (AH-dee-das). But in the United States, many people stress the second syllable instead (ah-DEE-das).

The complexities of sponsorships among leagues, teams, and players mean that some crossovers do happen. Athletes and their teams may receive endorsements from different companies. Lionel Messi, for example, wore

Adidas while playing for Barcelona, a Nike-sponsored team. Another soccer star, Cristiano Ronaldo, has long been signed with Nike, but on the field he appeared in Juventus team colors made by Adidas.

COLLEGE SPORTS

For a long time, Adidas and other sportswear companies were prevented from working with amateur athletes. In recent years that has begun to change. The National Collegiate Athletic Association (NCAA) runs college-level sports. The NCAA long banned players from earning endorsement money. The idea was that amateur college-level athletes should play for the love of the sport, not as paid professionals. Teams, however, could always earn money by using branded uniforms, shoes, and equipment.

A HEADY ENDORSEMENT

Quarterback Jim McMahon of the Chicago Bears carefully cultivated his image as a rebel during the 1980s. He stayed out late on game nights and broke other team rules. He even got in the face of Pete Rozelle, commissioner of the National Football League (NFL).

He did it just by wearing an Adidas headband. The NFL didn't mind headbands, and McMahon had an endorsement contract with the company. But the league forbade any visible company logos on clothing. Rozelle responded by fining the Bears $5,000. As usual, McMahon got the last laugh. For the conference championship game that year, he wore another headband, this one labeled "Rozelle."[4]

> *Star quarterback Patrick Mahomes is among the NFL players who lace up a pair of spiked Adidas shoes on game day.*

59

That changed in 2021, the year when the NCAA decided to allow individual athletes to sign for paid endorsements. With college athletes available, Adidas and other companies began exploring ways to work with them. When offering endorsement deals, they look for more than just stats and championships. Matt Powell, a sports industry adviser, explains: "It's all about personality, fashion style, and, obviously, performance on the field—it's a package of all those things."[5]

WEARING THE THREE STRIPES

PRODUCT SPOTLIGHT

In 1967, Adidas brought out its first nonshoe sportswear. The Adidas tracksuit was a comfortable, light outfit ideal for cooling down after a workout or a game. It came in a single color, with three white stripes running down the legs. When an Adidas tracksuit came into view, there could be no mistake about its maker—the three stripes gave it away.

To market the new tracksuit, the company enlisted Franz Beckenbauer, a star in the German soccer world. Beckenbauer appeared in Adidas print ads, lacing up his three-stripe Adidas shoes while wearing the matching sweatpants and top. Soccer and basketball players on both sides of the Atlantic began warming up in head-to-toe Adidas gear before matches.

The Adidas tracksuit helped to move sportswear into the fashion mainstream. Men, women, and kids who never went near a running track began wearing tracksuits in everyday life. The tracksuit was also ideal for jogging in cool weather and could be worn comfortably while working out. Adidas's tracksuits were ready for the mass market when the fitness craze hit in the 1980s.

CHAPTER SIX

ON THE ADIDAS TEAM

A didas supplies gear in addition to sponsoring individual athletes. The roster of Adidas-wearing leagues and teams is very long. It includes club soccer teams in Europe, US professional teams, and Olympic teams around the world. The company provides official gear for entire leagues, including the National Hockey League (NHL). It also sponsors broadcasts for teams and leagues, such as the European Women's Champions League.

Adidas has signed on as a sponsor in dozens of sports, including football, basketball, cricket, archery, volleyball, e-sports, snowboarding, handball, and golf. The company strives

> In 2015, the NHL and Adidas announced the signing of a long-term contract for Adidas to produce all of the league's uniforms.

to be a global brand recognized by everybody, no matter what team or sport they follow.

Adidas also sponsors events, including the biggest international soccer tournament of all, the FIFA World Cup, and smaller events such as the Easter Bowl championship for up-and-coming tennis players. There are Adidas basketball tournaments and marathons. Adidas has been the official footwear supplier to the famous Boston Marathon since 1989. It also makes Boston Marathon jackets and T-shirts for those who participate as runners or officials.

THE GROWTH OF SPONSORSHIP

Sponsorships have grown in value since Adi Dassler founded the company in the 1940s. When Dassler was young, not many athletes earned a lot of money as players, with just a few sports in Europe and the United States attracting

FACTORIES IN THE OPEN

Many companies that outsource production are secretive about their supply-chain partners. They may not want competitors to outbid them for work. They also may not want workers' rights organizations to put their partners' labor practices under examination.

Adidas claims to go the other way. On its website, the company names every factory it currently uses as a production source. Specific suppliers for particular events, including the European soccer championship, the FIFA World Cup, and the Olympic Games, are listed. A global list as of July 2021 included more than 500 factories by country, from Argentina to Vietnam, with the street address and the operating company given.[1]

The Adidas logo was seen on the soccer balls used for the 2022 FIFA World Cup European Qualifiers.

big crowds to stadiums. With television, which was just starting out in the late 1940s, the audience for sports grew into the billions worldwide. Today there is huge money involved in television and media deals for professional sports teams, which has driven an increase in sports sponsorships.

In some cases, sponsorship is a high-level negotiation carried out in corporate boardrooms. Everything is confidential until the deal is closed and the terms are announced. Secrecy is essential because Adidas competes with companies such as Nike, Converse, Under Armour, and Puma for major team sponsorships.

Adidas also guards its turf as the world's leading sponsor of soccer. Although Nike has tried to gain a larger share of this sport, Adidas remains number one in sales of soccer apparel and gear. In 2021, Adidas executives closed a deal to remain an official FIFA World Cup sponsor until the year 2030.

HOW TEAM SPONSORSHIP WORKS

Adidas has a five-tiered sponsorship structure for teams. The company divides its clients into A or "Elite" teams, B or "Premium" teams, Standard teams, Third-Party teams, and No Contract teams. The relationship the company has with teams in each tier is different. For No Contract teams, for example, Adidas acts simply as an equipment supplier. No money changes hands. Sponsorships like this can represent a major savings of money and time for those running the team. It's an important consideration when budgets are small.

Teams in the A tier are among the most popular and famous teams in the world. For Adidas, these sponsorships are all about reaching the vast market of fans for teams such as Real Madrid. The Spanish soccer club earns $134 million every year from Adidas.[2]

PROPOSING SPONSORSHIP

For midtier teams, sponsorship has to be requested. Adidas will not sign up just any team or event. Hopeful clients have to send company executives a written proposal, which includes the size of their fan base and the local audience for their games. They also have to provide numbers on their local media reach. How many people come to the games? How many fans watch them on television or listen to their games on the radio? How successful has the team been? Does it have any championships? Does it reach local or state tournaments? Adidas will also consider the social media following of the organization or event. The greater the number of followers, the greater a team's influence and the more attractive a sponsorship is to the company. The company

HOW THE PYRAMID WORKS

The sponsorship levels Adidas uses to rank different teams have a lot to do with how the company markets team gear. This varies with every sport. For European soccer, for example, teams at the A level are featured in all of the company's collections; their gear is featured everywhere Adidas is sold. Teams at the B level are included in Adidas catalogs around the world.

Standard teams have their jerseys, hats, and scarves sold only in club shops in the country where they play. Third-party teams sign branding deals with Adidas through a marketing agency. Teams can go up and down the pyramid over time. These shifts are not a small matter. The better merchandising offered to higher-ranking teams is worth big money to the teams and their players.

> Adidas has long been a prominent sponsor of the Boston Marathon.

will evaluate the team's or event's audience and check that it conforms with a demographic Adidas is trying to reach. For example, an e-sports tournament that attracts a million online viewers, all of them young and eager buyers of branded gear, just might make the cut.

Events and teams that get sponsored may get much more than shirts and shoes to wear. Adidas can provide cobranded products that display the team and company logo. It may collaborate on media content, such as promotional videos and press releases. It may promote the team or event through Adidas's corporate website or social media channels. For a local team, collaboration with a big company like Adidas can mean stronger engagement with its fans and community.

For Adidas, the relationship can bring some benefits as well. A baseball tournament, for example, might feature the Adidas name and logo on its signs, programs, advertising, and media releases. The tournament may also offer places for Adidas to sell and market its shoes and other goods. Like any good business deal, there are benefits for both sides.

THE CENTER OF IT ALL

Adidas has come a long way since its beginnings in the Dassler family laundry room in the 1920s. The company headquarters is now a sprawling corporate campus in Herzogenaurach. The headquarters includes showrooms, workshops, and advanced labs for experimenting with new sportswear tech. Still, hiring top talent to come to a small town in the middle of Germany can be tough. Designers may prefer to be near fashion and cultural centers.

To address this issue, Adidas expanded its offices in Portland, Oregon. This was seen as a major, trendy city where younger brand managers and designers wouldn't mind living. It was also a place where Adidas could keep an eye on its biggest competitor, Nike, which has its world headquarters nearby.

CHAPTER SEVEN

REACHING OUT TO CONSUMERS

Like many other companies in the apparel and fashion business, Adidas plans its marketing strategy well in advance. The purpose is to place the company on the cutting edge of new styles and new tastes among consumers. In 2015, Adidas executives laid out a five-year campaign called "Creating the New."[1] They planned to gear their advertising to websites and mobile platforms. They would also make use of social media services such as Twitter and Facebook.

The main idea was to connect Adidas more directly with individual customers. Through new applications and new technology, these shoppers and buyers would have a direct line to shoe designers. The company would strive

> As with many other brands, Adidas has made a strong effort to connect with customers online and through mobile devices.

▶ *The flagship Adidas store on Fifth Avenue in New York City features elaborate displays.*

to create excitement and buzz every time a new line of shoes or sportswear made an appearance.

STRATEGIC CITIES

As part of this strategy, the company focused its marketing effort on six major cities: London, Paris, Shanghai, Tokyo, New York City, and Los Angeles. Adidas sees these megacities as fashion and taste trendsetters for the rest of the world. While marketing in the European cities is focused on soccer equipment, the American cities would see more basketball and baseball gear.

Each of these key cities is home to an Adidas flagship store. The Adidas megastore in London is a vast space that lines busy Oxford Street. It offers four floors of Adidas products displayed over 26,900 square feet (2,500 sq m) of interior space.[2] Artwork, both physical and digital, fills the space. Most of the works are from local creators, making the store as much a sports-themed art gallery as a retail establishment.

Anyone planning a visit to the London store, or any Adidas store, can go online to figure out which products they'd like to see. They can use an online three-dimensional map to browse through the store. Once they arrive, they scan barcodes on products to find out whether their size is in stock or if it's on sale. If their size is available, they can scan and purchase on the spot, without waiting in a checkout line.

ADIDAS PARK

Adidas Park in the Dorchester/Roxbury neighborhood of Boston, Massachusetts, was once a nameless vacant lot, a place the locals used as a trash dump. That all changed in 1983, when an Adidas fan named Timothy White began clearing away the debris. He named the place after his favorite brand of shoe. Only Adidas shoes were allowed in Adidas Park. Not even top-of-the-line Nikes or Pumas made the cut. Anybody daring to enter with incorrect sneakers was at risk of getting beaten up and having their shoes removed. Offending pairs were hung on a tree. One local break-dancer recalled, "There was a tree there that had tons of shoes in it. It looked like a Christmas tree.... I never got caught up there, but heard many stories."[3]

TAKING A TEST RUN

In an Adidas flagship store, the fun really begins when a customer picks out a pair of new shoes and asks to try them on. Adidas has equipped its leading stores with high-tech treadmills, allowing shoppers a trial run in their shoes before they buy. In the London store, this area includes a huge video screen that shows city scenes that move along at the runner's own pace.

The fitting rooms are set up with scanners that read barcodes to discover exactly what the customer is trying on. A video screen in the booth makes suggestions on additional gear on sale in the store, and it also advises on sizes and colors that are in stock. The store includes dedicated rooms for cleaning

THE PRICE OF FAKE ADIDAS

Like other big companies, Adidas is very protective of its brand. It doesn't want anyone else copying or imitating its products. That would mean not only competition but also a loss of brand prestige for Adidas, which could do the company financial harm.

When shoe retailer Payless ShoeSource started making its own sneakers with two or four stripes, Adidas went to court, charging trademark infringement. The non-Adidas shoes sold for less, though they never got close to the popularity of the real thing. The case began in 2001 and continued through the court system until 2008, when a jury reached a unanimous verdict in favor of Adidas. The damages amounted to $305 million, at the time the largest award in any trademark case in history.[4]

> *People all over the world can browse and purchase Adidas shoes with a few taps on a phone.*

and repairing shoes, and tailors on staff work on apparel and accessories.

In its physical stores, Adidas also strives to project environmental awareness. Renewable energy powers the London store and others where possible. It's common for the various fixtures in the stores, including the benches, racks, mannequins, and cabinets, to be made from renewable materials.

ONLINE SHOPPING AND THE PANDEMIC

The COVID-19 pandemic that spread globally in early 2020 posed a serious challenge to Adidas and other apparel companies. In many locations, lockdowns prevented people from leaving their homes except for essential errands such as grocery shopping. Fitness centers and school gyms closed down, and sports leagues cut their schedules or canceled their seasons. This softened demand for athletic wear.

Adidas, along with many other companies, moved its operations online. The company expanded its online offerings, making it easier for customers to shop online and have their products delivered. This boosted sales at a time when physical outlets were struggling with light traffic, staff shortages, and shortened hours. Unable to bring its products to showrooms, Adidas also created digital showrooms

ADIDAS ON DISPLAY

The Adidas museum at the company headquarters in Herzogenaurach has an archive of more than 40,000 products.[5] The museum offers tours of the collection, and guides always wear white gloves to handle the products when presenting them. Adidas has appeared in other museums around the world too. The Metropolitan Museum of Art in New York, which has the biggest collection of art in the country, includes in its Costume Institute a pair of blue Adidas shoes made in 1972.

> *Like many other apparel companies, Adidas produced face masks during the COVID-19 pandemic.*

in order to stay linked to the wholesalers who distribute the company's products to stores. The wholesalers could go online to experience a three-dimensional virtual-reality app that displayed the new releases.

The pandemic was also the catalyst for several other digital innovations. The company started the Creators Club, a loyalty program that allowed users to log in and earn points by tracking their runs or workouts.

By collecting points for their exercise achievements, they received discounts on new Adidas gear.

SPEEDFACTORIES

In the 2010s, a new Adidas initiative was developed to quickly respond to sportswear trends. This led to the creation of Speedfactories in 2016. At these new manufacturing facilities in Europe and the United States, Adidas used robots to quickly construct new shoes, rather than making the products at traditional factories overseas.

This idea put multiple operations under a single roof, instead of having various suppliers provide the different shoe parts from different locations. This would cut down on manufacturing time and transport time to market. New designs could be rendered in three-dimensional design software, then swiftly put into production.

The Speedfactory idea was not a success, however. Making shoes is a complex operation, with dozens of cutting, shaping, and assembly steps along the way. Setting up robots to do the work is expensive and time-consuming. Adidas discovered that it cost more to produce shoes with robots than with humans, in part because overseas labor costs were low. The company closed its Speedfactory facilities in 2020.

SMART SHOES

PRODUCT SPOTLIGHT

Adidas has been installing computer technology in its shoes since 1985, when it introduced the Micropacer. This running shoe had a built-in computer that measured average speed, the length of the runner's stride, and the number of calories burned on a run or walk.

The original mission of the Adidas 1 "smart shoe," released in 2004, was to gauge how hard or soft the ground surface was. By measuring the surface, the shoe could adjust its cushioning to make the wearer's feet as comfortable as possible.

The company took smart shoe technology to a higher level in 2019 with the F50 Adizero shoe, designed for soccer superstar Lionel Messi. The miCoach chip in this shoe makes performance data, including speed, distance, stride length, step length, and sprint times, available in real time. With a wireless data connection built in, the Adizero with miCoach can send the information to a separate device. A coach with a laptop or iPad, for example, can follow player performance in real time. This gives the coach more data when considering adjustments or substitutions, improving the performance of the entire team.

CHAPTER EIGHT

CONTROVERSIES AND CHALLENGES

Controversy has swirled around the Dassler brothers and Adidas for generations. During the 1930s, both Adi and Rudolf were members of the brutal Nazi Party, which took power in Germany in 1933. Their feud over the company's political allegiances, and their own wartime service in the German military, split the brothers and led to the founding of Adidas by Adi Dassler in 1949.

When it was a young and growing company, Adidas's major controversies involved the Olympic Games. In 1972, the Summer Games returned to West Germany, which hosted the Olympics in the city of Munich. This Bavarian city is not far from Herzogenaurach. By this time, Horst

> Adidas and its founder, Adi Dassler, have attracted controversy throughout the company's history.

Dassler, the son of Adi Dassler, had joined the company and was traveling around the world to promote Adidas. He saw the Games as an opportunity to promote a new product line: Adidas sportswear.

To Adi, the idea of branching out into clothing was a nonstarter. His family's company had started by making shoes. In his opinion, it should sell only shoes. But Horst belonged to a new generation. He saw that sports and leisure fashion were merging. More people were giving exercise and sports an important place in their lives. They formed a huge new market for sportswear that Adidas could reach.

The IOC opposed any commercial promotion at the Games. It didn't want athletes showing the names of commercial sponsors. It also banned the Adidas name from appearing on any team clothing. The controversy was another installment in the long-running debate around amateurism at the Olympic Games.

NOT GETTING ALONG

The rivalry between Puma and Adidas forever marked the town of Herzogenaurach. Townspeople felt the rivalry as a constant, divisive presence. Many of them joined one camp or the other, depending on the shoes they wore, the company they kept, or the place where they worked. When an outsider came to visit, townspeople always looked down to check what brand of shoes was being worn. As a result of this practice, Herzogenaurach became known as the Town of Bent Necks.

> American marathon winner Frank Shorter was among the athletes at the 1972 Munich Olympics wearing the iconic Adidas stripes.

However, the IOC at Munich did allow tracksuits displaying the three white stripes. Horst also persuaded the committee to allow a new logo to appear on team jerseys. For this purpose Adidas used its new trefoil design. The company featured the trefoil prominently in its advertising. Most people who saw the logo on clothing worn by Olympic wrestlers, gymnasts, and runners knew what it represented.

Horst had a talent for getting around rules. He knew about the strict ban on selling any sporting goods on Olympic grounds. So Adidas set up a large tent in Munich to promote its merchandise. The tent had a room at the back stocked with company products. Adidas representatives spread the word among athletes that the company would make its spikes available to Olympic athletes, free for the asking.

PROBLEMS WITH THE NCAA

Through the 1960s and 1970s, Adidas branched out into college sports marketing. But promoting a company through college-level athletics is a very different challenge from marketing with professional sports. College athletes could earn scholarships but not direct pay or endorsements. However, some college sports programs were highly visible and brought in a lot of money. This created a disconnect between the athletes and the money they generated for schools.

Adidas and other sports apparel companies sometimes took advantage of the situation. Adidas sponsored certain college teams, and it was in their interest for those teams to be successful. So in the 2010s the company arranged gifts, including cash, to talented high school players. Although such gifts are not against the law, they do break NCAA rules against any form of paid recruitment. Adidas also arranged payments to college players through team coaches and assistants.

Three men, including two Adidas executives, were charged with wire fraud for this scheme. The federal prosecutors in the case accused the defendants of arranging payments from Adidas to the players and hiding them from the schools—thus convincing the schools to issue scholarships under false pretenses. One such payment amounted to $100,000 to the father of Brian "Tugs" Bowen, who signed with the University of Louisville basketball team.[1]

The three men pled innocent to the charges, then were put on trial together. After three weeks of hearing testimony and evidence, the

OLD NEWS IN COLLEGE HOOPS

At first, the collegiate basketball scandal that erupted in 2018 was known as the Adidas recruiting scandal, as Adidas was the first company mentioned by investigators. Eventually, many more companies found themselves involved. Adidas wasn't the only one offering payments to players through their coaches and agents, and the practice was common knowledge among everybody involved with the college game.

College coaches did what they could to give their teams an edge. This meant getting good players by any means possible, even if it meant breaking NCAA rules. A famous quote attributed to legendary college coach Jerry Tarkanian summed it all up: "Nine out of ten schools are cheating; the other one is in last place."[2]

jury found them guilty and sentenced each of the men to a few months in prison.

THE PROBLEM WITH SWEATSHOPS

Adidas has also faced controversy over the use of sweatshops and child labor. Like many clothing and shoe companies, Adidas contracts with suppliers who run factories in poor and developing countries, many of them in Asia. For sewing clothing and assembling shoes, these factories pay far less than similar jobs in North America and Europe. Such facilities may demand long hours, have unhealthy working conditions, and hire young children to do the work.

Adidas and similar companies, such as Nike and Puma, are aware of criticism over the issue but feel they have no choice. If a competitor can save money on labor, it will have more money to spend on marketing and advertising. It will also have a bigger budget for research, design, and sponsorships. The financial advantage will translate into better market share, and a loss of income and profitability for the competition.

To meet public criticism over factory conditions, Adidas joined the Fair Labor Association (FLA). The FLA sets down guidelines for working conditions and wages.

> *A worker assembles Adidas shoes at a factory in China in 2005.*

Wages, for example, are supposed to provide a worker with the ability to meet basic needs such as housing, food, water, transportation, clothing, and health care. On its website, Adidas declares that its suppliers can never hire children under the age of 15. If the local age for completing required education is above 15, people must be at least that age to work for an Adidas supplier.

DOING RIGHT IN HARD TIMES

The COVID-19 pandemic caused problems for many businesses, including the sportswear business. Adidas and other companies saw a downturn in sales to consumers and a drop in orders from distributors. For factories in Asia, the pandemic caused thousands of order cancellations. This led to a drastic drop in payments. Some companies simply refused to pay for any orders, even if the finished merchandise was ready to ship. To cope with the loss of income, factories began firing or laying off their workers.

The result was more hardship for low-wage factory workers in poor countries and bad publicity for companies refusing to pay for their finished goods. Adidas, however, has long been sensitive to its image as a company that depends on overseas labor. The company made a public commitment to pay in full for any order completed by its factories.

BOYCOTTS IN CHINA

Adidas has faced a different labor controversy in China. This huge nation of more than one billion people is controlled by the Chinese Communist Party. The government strictly enforces laws against any opposition to its rule within China. It also responds quickly and forcefully to any criticism on the part of foreign governments or companies.

Most Chinese cotton comes from the Xinjiang region, located in the far northwestern corner of China. Members of an ethnic minority known as the Uighurs live in this region. China's treatment of this minority, including detaining

> *Adidas has been popular in China, but political controversies harmed the brand's standing there.*

GIVING BACK

Adidas has been involved in charitable programs around the world for many years. The company and its employees contribute money and volunteer hours, focusing on countries where it sources shoes and clothing. Adidas also donates its products to community sports programs in Latin America, Europe, the Middle East, and Asia.

During the COVID-19 pandemic, Adidas and a partner company, Carbon, manufactured face shields at the rate of 18,000 per week using 3D printing technology. The company offered a 30 percent discount on its products to first responders and medical personnel, and it donated $3.25 million to the Solidarity Response Fund supporting the World Health Organization.[4] The company also announced it would match donations to COVID relief programs made by its employees.

people and moving them to what the government calls "re-education camps," has drawn global criticism.[3] With the consent of the Chinese government, cotton producers rely on forced labor among the Uighurs to make raw cotton for clothing, including clothing sold by Adidas.

When Adidas expressed opposition to this practice, it sparked a revolt among consumers in China. The Chinese government denied the charges of forced labor. It rallied citizens to boycott Adidas products and instead buy their sportswear from Anta, a Chinese company. Huawei, a big Chinese telecommunications company, removed Adidas apps from its app store.

The boycott has cost Adidas. The brand was barred from selling its products on big Chinese shopping sites such as Alibaba and Taobao, causing a major hit to sales in the world's most populous market. But the company also must respond to public criticism in other countries, where people see the Uighurs as unfairly exploited.

As the Xinjiang issue shows, Adidas is more than a sportswear company. It's an international brand that, at least since the Berlin Olympics, has been involved in contentious politics and thorny social issues.

CHAPTER NINE

MARKETING THREE STRIPES

Adidas, like other large companies, spends a large sum on marketing its products and defining itself in the public eye. It has expressed its mission as simply "to be the best sports brand in the world."[1] But it also defines itself as a shoe company and still focuses its innovation and new technology on athletic shoes. Within the footwear segment, Adidas has tried to reduce the number of different models and focus on developing key shoe lines such as the Superstar, the Samba, and the Stan Smith. This concept extends to notable apparel lines including Tiro training pants, the Z.N.E. hoodie, and the MyShelter jacket.

Adidas has also made outreach to women a part of its marketing strategy.

> *An enormous Adidas advertisement appeared on a building in Berlin in 2014.*

FUTURE SHOES

Athletes play a major role at Future Lab, Adidas's research and development facility in Germany. The company brings pros to the lab and puts them through a battery of motions and workouts. Scanners and sensors take measurements down to a microscopic scale. In the quest for optimal comfort and durability, this research and development work has resulted in the improvement of many shoe components.

The tradition goes back to Adi Dassler, who took great pride in his genius for tinkering, experimenting, and inventing. By the time of his death, the founder and his company had created or acquired hundreds of patents in the design, materials, and manufacturing of sports shoes.

The company makes women's footwear, running tights, and sports bras. It has also come out with a line of mastectomy bras designed for female athletes returning to sports after breast cancer surgery.

As part of this outreach, Adidas developed the She Breaks Barriers public service campaign. There were several different components of the campaign. Adidas joined the Global Sport Institute, a research institute, to work on overcoming barriers to women's participation in sports. The company also sponsored the Women's National Football Conference and projects in New York and Los Angeles to help girls and women take part in local sports events and leagues. With the support of Adidas, Jen Welter, the first female coach in NFL history, started girls' flag football camps to get more school-age girls involved in the sport.

PARTNERING WITH THE STARS

Partnerships with global pop culture icons are also important parts of the Adidas strategy. The company has signed with Bad Bunny and Pharrell Williams to create new editions of its franchise lines. It strives to create buzz by working with hot designers, including Prada and the menswear label Wales Bonner.

Adidas defines its leading promoters and endorsers as a Creator Network. These are stars such as Kanye West and Beyoncé, who do far more for the company than wear its gear and appear in its advertising. They collaborate on new lines of shoes and clothing, lending personal and popular style to Adidas products.

Even for a large company like Adidas, marketing budgets are limited, so the

SHOES IN SPACE

Creators is the term Adidas uses to identify people who partner with the company to design or promote its products. Creators aren't limited to pop stars and athletes, however. Adidas has also set up a partnership with the US National Laboratory aboard the International Space Station (ISS). This enormous orbiting spacecraft hosts astronauts from many different countries to carry out experiments and make observations in orbit 250 miles (400 km) above Earth.

Adidas arranged to have ISS astronauts perform an experiment on its Boost technology in microgravity. In the space environment, a high-speed camera tracked the movement and arrangement of the tiny pellets that make up Boost midsoles. The ultimate goal was to help designers improve the shoe's performance back on Earth.

company must set priorities for its spending. For events, it concentrates promotion on those that draw international participation, such as the World Cup and high-profile marathons in Boston and Berlin. It also favors partnerships with major teams, including national soccer teams in Europe and Latin America, and the clubs with the biggest fan bases, such as Manchester United, Real Madrid, Arsenal, Bayern Munich, and Juventus.

A SUSTAINABLE BRAND

Adidas also sees sustainability as an important branding and marketing goal. The company uses recycled materials in several product lines. The Infinite Hoodie, designed by designer Stella McCartney, is fully recyclable. A new Futurecraft Loop 2 shoe is made by grinding up and reusing materials from Futurecraft Loop 1 shoes. A takeback program is in place for buyers to return and recycle their used

PLAYING FOR A NEW TEAM

Top athletes in solo sports, such as tennis and golf, can have their pick of endorsement deals. The Japanese tennis player Naomi Osaka signed an Adidas sponsorship while still relatively unknown. With a frightening first serve clocked at 125 miles per hour (201 kmh), she rocketed to stardom after beating Serena Williams to win the 2018 US Open championship.[2] In 2019, she abruptly dropped Adidas to sign a contract with Nike that paid her approximately $10 million a year.[3]

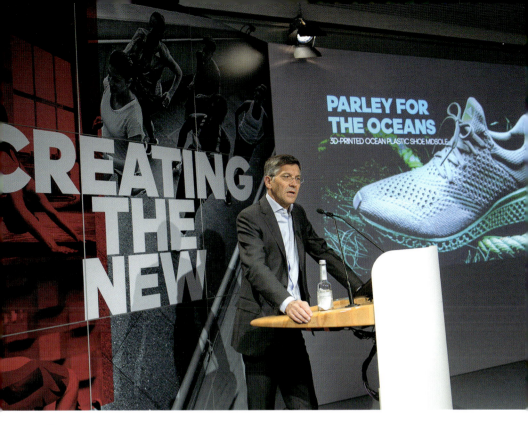

▶ *Adidas CEO Herbert Hainer introduced the Parley shoe at a 2016 news conference.*

gear. The Parley line of shoes is made with plastic waste recovered from the oceans. Adidas also strives to use renewable energy sources in its stores and factories.

In 2020, the company also set itself an ambitious goal of becoming a carbon-neutral organization by 2050.[4] This means offsetting the emissions that the company's activities generate. A carbon-neutral company thus benefits the effort to stabilize Earth's warming climate and also benefits its own image as environmentally aware and active.

OWNING THE GAME

Every five years, Adidas develops a new marketing theme and campaign. The purpose is to adjust the company's goals and themes to improve public perception of the brand. In 2020, the new Own the Game campaign was rolled out.

Own the Game expanded the company's focus on strategic cities by adding Mexico City, Seoul, Moscow, Dubai, Berlin, and Beijing. These were places where style trends were being set and large, concentrated markets could be reached with messaging, stores, and advertising. Adidas announced new efforts to reach a mass consumer market in rapidly growing parts of Europe, the Middle East, Africa, and Asia.

As part of this new campaign, Adidas concentrates on direct-to-consumer (DTC) sales and digital platforms. Recognizing that most sportswear buyers have gone digital, the company sought to personalize the experience of shopping for new gear online or via mobile platforms. The company set up a Creators Club membership program in 2018, with the goal of making the shopping experience direct and personal. Using a point system, members are rewarded for their engagement and purchases with access to limited editions, special events, and product promotional sales. Adidas wants to reach a total worldwide membership of 500 million by 2025. It also aims for DTC accounting for half of total sales.[5]

The personal connection is meant to take place in stores as well, with personalized fitting and sampling of shoes and other products. Adidas wants a reputation as a high-tech sports brand catering to the preferences, sports, ages, and tastes of all its customers.

GETTING THE PLASTIC OUT

Adidas has taken on the problem of plastic waste dumped into Earth's oceans. It's not a small problem. Truckloads of plastic are dumped offshore every day, with much of the material winding up as litter on seacoasts and the beaches of remote islands. By one estimate, by 2050 there'll be more plastic than fish by weight in the seas.[6]

To tackle this problem, Adidas began a collaboration in 2015 with Parley, an environmental group dedicated to repairing the damage to the oceans from dumping plastic waste. Adidas developed a new material known as Parley Ocean Plastic, made from plastic waste found on coastal land. The plastic is shredded and worked into polyester yarn that goes into Parley shoes and sportswear.

ESSENTIAL FACTS

KEY EVENTS

- Brothers Adolf (Adi) and Rudolf Dassler found the Dassler Brothers Sports Shoe Factory in 1924 in their hometown of Herzogenaurach, Germany.

- At the Berlin Summer Olympics in 1936, US athlete Jesse Owens wins gold medals in four events wearing the Dassler brothers' shoes.

- In 1949, Adi Dassler establishes Adidas.

- In 1952, Adidas buys the three-stripe logo from Karhu, a Finnish shoe company.

- In 1972, Adidas unveils its trefoil logo at the Munich Summer Olympics.

- On the death of Adi Dassler in 1978, his wife Käthe runs the company. When she dies in 1984, their son Horst takes over Adidas.

- In 1986, rap group Run-DMC signs an endorsement deal with Adidas.

- Adidas opens a high-tech flagship store in New Delhi, the capital of India, in 2021.

KEY PEOPLE

- Adi Dassler cofounds a shoe company in the 1920s with his brother Rudolf, then splits with Rudolf to start Adidas in 1949.

- Rudolf Dassler founds the rival sports shoe company Puma after a split with his brother Adi.

- Horst Dassler, the son of Adi Dassler, takes control of Adidas after his mother dies in 1984. Horst was a talented and energetic businessman in his own right, and he plays a founding role in the business of athletic product endorsements.

- Robert Louis-Dreyfus, the French chairman of Adidas, puts the company on a successful path while leading the company starting in 1993.

KEY PRODUCTS

- Stan Smith: Named for a champion tennis player from the United States, this simple, white low-rise shoe has been Adidas's best-selling product for decades.

- Superstar: Developed in the 1960s, this basketball shoe has a shell toe and a leather upper, protecting the toes and giving players a greater ability to push off and to pivot.

- Telstar: This soccer ball was introduced in the 1960s to make the ball more visible during matches and has become the most recognizable design for soccer balls at all levels of the sport.

- Tracksuit: This simple but very practical outfit, Adidas's first effort in nonshoe sports apparel, was ideal for warm-ups and became a favorite among sports fans around the world.

QUOTE

"Innovate, don't imitate."

—*Adi Dassler*

GLOSSARY

cinder track
A running track made of small rock fragments mixed with dirt and ash.

conglomerate
A large company that owns multiple smaller companies that may operate independently.

direct-to-consumer
Selling goods through online or mobile platforms, without using salespeople or a physical space such as a store.

endorsement
A public recommendation or suggestion to use a certain product.

ethylene-vinyl acetate
A tough, rubberlike compound used to cushion midsoles of shoes made by Adidas and other brands.

last
A wooden form in the shape of a foot used to make shoes by hand.

logo
A simple design appearing on products and advertising that represents a company.

pitch
The field on which soccer matches are played.

royalty
A payment made to athletes, as a percentage of sales, for the use of their names on a product.

spike
A thin metal point on the bottom of a sports shoe, designed to improve surface grip.

thermoplastic polyurethane
A plastic compound that can be ground up and recycled into new shoes.

tracksuit
A single-color athletic outfit composed of a shirt and sweatpants.

trefoil
A design with a shape that has three parts.

upper
In shoe design, the part of the shoe that covers the foot above the sole.

ADDITIONAL RESOURCES

SELECTED BIBLIOGRAPHY

Karlsch, Rainer. *Playing the Game: The History of Adidas*. Prestel, 2019.

Smit, Barbara. *Sneaker Wars: The Enemy Brothers Who Founded Adidas and Puma and the Family Feud That Forever Changed the Business of Sports*. Ecco, 2009.

Smith, Stan. *Some People Think I'm a Shoe*. Rizzoli, 2018.

FURTHER READINGS

Jaskulka, Marie. *Puma*. Abdo, 2023.

McKinney, Donna. *Excelling in Soccer*. ReferencePoint, 2020.

Mooney, Carla. *Nike*. Abdo, 2023.

ONLINE RESOURCES

To learn more about Adidas, please visit **abdobooklinks.com** or scan this QR code. These links are routinely monitored and updated to provide the most current information available.

MORE INFORMATION

For more information on this subject, contact or visit the following organizations:

ADIDAS AG HEADQUARTERS
Adi-Dassler-Strasse 1
91074 Herzogenaurach
Germany
adidas-group.com/en/about/headquarters/
+49-9132840

The huge Adidas campus in the hometown of the Dassler brothers houses 5,600 employees. There's a museum of Adidas history on-site, as well as a soccer pitch, tennis courts, a running track, and beach volleyball courts.

ADIDAS STORE NYC
565 Fifth Ave.
New York, NY 10017
fifthavenue.nyc/adidas
212-883-5606

The four-story flagship store, rising behind a wall of steel and glass, is a colorful, multimedia stadium of sportswear, with features designed to give visitors the look and feel of a bustling high school sports complex.

US OLYMPIC AND PARALYMPIC MUSEUM
200 S. Sierra Madre St.
Colorado Springs, CO 80903
usopm.org
719-497-1234

This museum is dedicated to US Olympic and Paralympic athletes and features artifacts, media, and technology related to the members of Team USA.

SOURCE NOTES

CHAPTER 1. THE HOME OF POSSIBILITIES
  1. "Adidas Opens Flagship Store in Delhi for a Seamless Shopping Experience." *India News Republic*, 29 Sept. 2021, indianewsrepublic.com. Accessed 18 Feb. 2022.
  2. "Adidas Opens Flagship Store in Delhi."
  3. "Leading Sportswear Giant Adidas Launches First Flagship Store in India." *Business Standard*, 15 Sept. 2021, business-standard.com. Accessed 18 Feb. 2022.

CHAPTER 2. THE STARTING LINE
  1. "Lina Radke." *Encyclopedia Britannica*, 10 Feb. 2022, britannica.com. Accessed 18 Feb. 2022.
  2. "Eleven Wretched Women." *University of Delaware: Engineering Exercise and Sports*, 21 Feb. 2018, sites.udel.edu. Accessed 18 Feb. 2022.
  3. "Chronicle and Biography of Adi & Käthe Dassler." *Adi & Käthe Dassler Memorial Foundation*, 2022, adidassler.org. Accessed 18 Feb. 2022.
  4. Von Robert Kuhn and Thomas Thiel. "The Prehistory of Adidas and Puma." *Spiegel International*, 4 Mar. 2009, spiegel.de. Accessed 18 Feb. 2022.
  5. Matilda Egere-Cooper. "Jesse Owens: Light in the Darkness." *Runners World*, 14 Oct. 2021, runnersworld.com. Accessed 18 Feb. 2022.

CHAPTER 3. WARTIME DEFEAT, OLYMPIC VICTORIES
  1. Barbara Smit. *Sneaker Wars*. Harper Perennial, 2009. 18.
  2. "Adi's Quotes." *Adi & Käthe Dassler Memorial Foundation*, 2022, adidassler.org. Accessed 18 Feb. 2022.
  3. Tim Newcomb. "The History of the Swoosh on Nike's Sneakers." *Complex*, 9 Mar. 2021, complex.com. Accessed 18 Feb. 2022.

CHAPTER 4. NEW SHOES, NEW STYLES

1. Andrew Flint. "João Havelange: The Iron Hand in an Iron Glove." *These Football Times*, 30 May 2015, thesefootballtimes.co. Accessed 18 Feb. 2022.

2. Gary Warnett. "How Run-DMC Earned Their Adidas Stripes." *Mr Porter*, 27 May 2016, mrporter.com. Accessed 18 Feb. 2022.

3. Seb Joseph. "Why Adidas Treats Esports Deals Like Media Partnerships, Not Sponsorship Deals." *Digiday*, 18 Jan. 2021, digiday.com. Accessed 18 Feb. 2022.

4. Joseph, "Why Adidas Treats Esports Deals Like Media Partnerships."

CHAPTER 5. WORKING WITH ATHLETES

1. "3. David Beckham." *AskMen*, n.d., askmen.com. Accessed 18 Feb. 2022.

2. Aaron Chow. "Lionel Messi's PSG Jersey Sold Out in Just 30 Minutes." *Hypebeast*, 12 Aug. 2021, hypebeast.com. Accessed 18 Feb. 2022.

3. Kate Krosschell. "Adidas Case Story: Athlete Performance with the Right Emotional Fit in Footwear—Featuring Jeff Goldblum." *Imotions*, 14 Sept. 2021, imotions.com. Accessed 18 Feb. 2022.

4. "Headband Isn't a Laughing Matter; $5,000 Fine Stands." *Los Angeles Times*, 14 Jan. 1986, latimes.com. Accessed 18 Feb. 2022.

5. Peter Verry. "College Athletes Can Now Benefit from Their Name, Image & Likeness—But Should Shoe Brands Rush to Invest?" *Footwear News*, 1 July 2021, footwearnews.com. Accessed 18 Feb. 2022.

CHAPTER 6. ON THE ADIDAS TEAM

1. "Global Factory Lists." *Adidas Group*, n.d., adidas-group.com. Accessed 18 Feb. 2022.

2. Siddharth Muruga. "Biggest Sponsorship Deals in Football Right Now 2022." *Sporting Free*, 17 Apr. 2021, sportingfree.com. Accessed 18 Feb. 2022.

SOURCE NOTES CONTINUED

CHAPTER 7. REACHING OUT TO CONSUMERS

1. Arthur Friedman. "Adidas CEO Says 'Creating the New' Initiative Making Strides." *Sourcing Journal*, 11 May 2018, sourcingjournal.com. Accessed 18 Feb. 2022.

2. "The Blending of Physical and Digital, Adidas and Razer Reinvent Physical Store Experience." *Spinoso*, 16 Oct. 2020, spinosoreg.com. Accessed 18 Feb. 2022.

3. "Three for the Stripes: Friends, Family, Boston." *Bodega*, n.d., bdgastore.com. Accessed 18 Feb. 2022.

4. Thomas J. Ryan. "Adidas Wins $305 Million Verdict against Collective Brands." *SGB Media*, 6 May 2008, sgbonline.com. Accessed 18 Feb. 2022.

5. Tim Newcomb. "Inside the Adidas Archives in Germany: The White Glove Treatment for 40,000 Meaningful Products." *Forbes*, 21 Nov. 2019, forbes.com. Accessed 18 Feb. 2022.

CHAPTER 8. CONTROVERSIES AND CHALLENGES

1. "Adidas Executive and Two Others Convicted of Defrauding Adidas-Sponsored Universities in Connection with Athletic Scholarships." *US Attorney's Office, Southern District of New York*, 24 Oct. 2018, justice.gov. Accessed 18 Feb. 2022.

2. Doug Robinson. "New Documentary: Adidas Recruiting Scandal Amounted to Nothing." *Deseret News*, 8 Apr. 2020, deseret.com. Accessed 18 Feb. 2022.

3. "Who Are the Uyghurs and Why Is China Being Accused of Genocide?" *BBC News*, 21 June 2021, bbc.com. Accessed 18 Feb. 2022.

4. "COVID-19." *Adidas*, n.d., adidas.com. Accessed 18 Feb. 2022.

CHAPTER 9. MARKETING THREE STRIPES

1. "Adidas Brand Strategy." *Adidas Annual Report*, 2019, report.adidas-group.com. Accessed 18 Feb. 2022.

2. Madilyn Zeegers. "Who Had the Fastest Serve in Women's Tennis?" *Sportscasting*, 13 July 2019, sportscasting.com. Accessed 18 Feb. 2022.

3. Tim Newcomb. "Naomi Osaka Switches Course, Inks Nike Endorsement Deal." *Forbes*, 3 Apr. 2019, forbes.com. Accessed 18 Feb. 2022.

4. Katja Schreiber. "Carbon Neutrality at Adidas: How Our Sustainability Strategy Will Get Us There." *GamePlan A*, 28 Oct. 2021, gameplan-a.com. Accessed 18 Feb. 2022.

5. "Strategy." Adidas, n.d., adidas-group.com. Accessed 18 Feb. 2022.

6. Sarah Kaplan. "By 2050, There Will Be More Plastic than Fish in the World's Oceans, Study Says." *Washington Post*, 20 January 2016, washingtonpost.com. Accessed 18 Feb. 2022.

INDEX

Abdul-Jabbar, Kareem, 47
Adicolor, 50–51
Adidas museum, 76
Adidas Park, 73
Auberge du Kochersberg, 48
Aurach River, 29

basketball, 6, 7, 28, 38–39, 42, 47, 56–57, 61, 63, 64, 72, 85
Beamon, Bob, 35
Beckenbauer, Franz, 61
Beckham, David, 55
Beyoncé, 7, 8, 95
Boston Marathon, 64
boycotts, 90–91

charity, 90
China, 25, 88–91
college basketball scandal, 84–86
college sports, 59–60, 84–86
Copa Mundial, 50
COVID-19 pandemic, 76–77, 88, 90
Creators Club, 77, 98

Dassler, Adolf (Adi), 11–12, 16–17, 19, 21, 26–29, 32, 34, 35, 53, 57, 81
Dassler, Horst, 31–32, 34, 35, 45, 54, 81–84
Dassler, Käthe, 35
Dassler, Rudolf, 12, 17, 26–29, 81
Dassler Brothers Sports Shoe Factory, 17, 26, 29, 53
Dollinger, Marie, 15

endorsements, 10–11, 45, 48–49, 55–60, 84, 95, 96
e-sports, 51, 63, 68

Fair Labor Association, 86
FIFA World Cup, 8, 29–30, 45, 50, 64, 66, 96
Future Lab, 94

Gupta, Sunil, 6

Hary, Armin, 34
Herzogenaurach, Germany, 16, 18, 28–29, 69, 76, 81, 82
Hitler, Adolf, 22

International Olympic Committee (IOC), 16, 82–83
International Space Station (ISS), 95
Ivy Park, 7, 8

Karhu, 32
Knight, Phil, 37

Louis-Dreyfus, Robert, 37

marketing, 10–12, 34, 45, 51, 71–73, 84, 86, 93–96, 98
McCartney, Stella, 7, 96
McMahon, Jim, 59
Messi, Lionel, 55–57, 79
Miracle of Bern, 29–31

National Football League (NFL), 59, 94
National Hockey League (NHL), 63
Nazi Germany, 12, 22, 28, 81
New Delhi, India, 5–7
Nike, 8, 10, 37, 41, 51, 59, 65–66, 69, 73, 86, 96
Nizza, 49

Olympics, 11, 15–16, 21–23, 28, 31–35, 54, 64, 81–84, 91
online shopping, 56, 73, 76–77, 98
Originals stores, 42
Osaka, Naomi, 96
Owens, Jesse, 23

plastic waste, 97, 99
Portland, Oregon, 69
Puma, 8, 29, 34, 35, 41, 48, 65, 73, 82, 86

Radke, Lina, 15–16, 21, 53
Reebok, 12
Run-DMC, 10, 47–48

Samba, 43, 93
Severn, Chris and Clifford, 34–35
smart shoes, 79
soccer, 7, 8, 13, 29–31, 43, 45, 50, 53, 55, 59, 61, 64, 66, 72, 79, 96
social media, 57, 67, 69, 71
Speedfactories, 78
spiked shoes, 16, 19–20, 21, 23, 32, 42
Spitz, Mark, 54
Stallone, Sylvester, 10
Stan Smith, 45–47, 54, 93
stores, 5–7, 41–42, 72–75, 97
strategic cities, 72, 98
Superstar, 38, 47, 49, 93
supply chains, 64
sustainability, 7, 12, 47, 96–97
sweatshops, 86

Tapie, Bernard, 35–36
team sponsorships, 8, 63–69, 84
Telstar soccer ball, 13
three stripes, 10, 21, 32–34, 41, 42, 61
Tobacco, 50
tracksuits, 42, 54, 61, 83
trefoil logo, 41, 83
Turman, Glynn, 8

Welter, Jen, 94
West, Kanye, 7, 54
World War I, 16, 18, 23
World War II, 25, 28, 29

ABOUT THE AUTHOR

TOM STREISSGUTH

Tom Streissguth has published more than 100 books of nonfiction for young people, including histories, biographies, current events books, and geography books. He started his own publishing company, The Archive, in 2015 to gather many of these hard-to-find literary works into multivolume collections. He has traveled widely in Asia, Europe, and the Middle East and has worked as a teacher and editor. Born in Washington, DC, he grew up in the Twin Cities area of Minnesota, where he currently lives.

ABOUT THE CONSULTANT

KHALID BALLOULI

Khalid Ballouli is an associate professor and PhD program director in the Department of Sport and Entertainment Management at the University of South Carolina. He received his BS, MS, and PhD in sport management from Texas A&M University. Ballouli's research interests center on sport marketing and sport consumer behavior. He was recently elected president of the Sport Marketing Association, and he currently serves on the editorial board for *Sport Marketing Quarterly*.

Prior to becoming an academic, Ballouli spent six years in professional baseball as a pitcher in the Milwaukee Brewers farm system, during which time he gained first-hand knowledge of the professional sports industry. He played college baseball at Texas A&M University, where he was a team captain, All-Conference, and NCAA College World Series participant. Ballouli remains active in his community by helping youth baseball organizations foster athlete and community development, and he often lends his time and expertise to researchers and educators in this field. Ballouli is married to Jessica, and they have four children, Farrah, Zaki, Maya, and Zayn.